HE MARRIED A WHORE WITH DADDY ISSUES

HE MARRIED A WHORE WITH DADDY ISSUES

Aimee Bilger

Charleston, SC
www.PalmettoPublishing.com

Paperback ISBN: 979-8-8229-3472-6

DEDICATION

This book is dedicated to my mother, Glenda. For over a decade, she has pushed me to write this book. In 2022, she stated, "Aimee, I want to see your book before I leave this earth." Because of your push, I can say, "It's complete, Momma." You are my best friend…even typing this, I'm getting teary-eyed because you absolutely mean the world to me. You did all you could possibly do to raise Scott and me to respect each other, people, and ourselves. We were functionally dysfunctional, but you always made sure we had everything we needed. There were times that you, as a single mother, didn't eat, just to make sure we did. You shopped for your clothes at yard sales and would buy ours from the mall. You disciplined us and loved us at the same time. As teens, we focused more on what you didn't do. As adults, we realized you did more than enough. You have been my listening ear, my laughing buddy, my recipe-giving encourager and motivator. Jeremy agrees that this dedication is well deserved. He appreciates you for being my person through my struggles. The Bilger family loves you, and we're thankful that God gave us *you*!

TABLE OF CONTENTS

CHAPTER 1
A FATHER'S LOVE

My first memory of my dad is of him pulling up to my grandmother's apartment on Melrose Street. Someone said, "Aimee, your daddy is here." My mom picked me up and carried me to this huge navy blue truck with big tires. The truck had a suspension lift. She had to extend me upward to hand me to him. I faintly remember smelling the scent of leather. He was wearing shades, black, shiny leather gloves, and a leather jacket. His jacket made a squeaky noise every time he moved. I knew I loved this man. He reached over to the passenger side and gave me a yellow box. I don't remember exactly what he said, but I remember his mouth moving. I felt like the conversation had something to do with the yellow box. When my mother came back to the truck, he kissed me and handed me back to her. As we approached my grandmother's porch, someone said, "Spoiled self," and laughed. My mom opened the yellow box and said the gift was a computer. It was a Speak & Read children's learning game. I played with it every day.

My second memory of Dad is of me and one of my older cousins walking down the street. She said, "Your dad is at home. I need you to go in and tell him you need some money." This was the moment I realized I didn't even know that my dad lived one street over from my grandmother's house. I began to wonder why I couldn't see him more often. I began to walk faster. When we arrived at the door, my cousin knocked. My dad came to the door, and I vaguely remember my cousin telling him who we were. I remember going inside the house, but my cousin stayed outside. An older lady was in the house. She asked me if I wanted some pancakes. I was overjoyed. I loved pancakes even though eating them would upset my stomach. I sat down at this small table that was placed against the wall in their kitchen. She gave me a plate of pancakes and a cup of coffee. I remember her sitting at the table with me. She began to ask me random questions about the food and how it tasted. She said, "You can call me Miss Mary." Then she asked me where my mother was. I told her that I didn't know and had come there with my cousin. My dad finally came up the hallway into the kitchen. He never acknowledged me. I felt like something was wrong, but I didn't know why. There was a weird, awkward feeling between Miss Mary and my dad. It was as if they were upset with each other. I remember looking at him and repeating what my cousin had told me to say. "Daddy, I need some money." He responded, "Did your momma send you here to ask for money?" I told him, "No, my cousin told me to ask you for some money." He looked at Miss

Mary, reached into his pocket, and gave me a few dollars, and I left. My cousin was still waiting outside. She asked me if I had gotten a chance to meet Miss Mary. She told me that Miss Mary was my other grandmother. This was mind-blowing to me. I didn't realize I had two grandmothers—and why didn't Miss Mary say that she was my grandmother? Why did I have to call her Miss Mary?

The third memory took place not too long after the day I sat at the table and ate pancakes. My brother and I had on what I considered clothes for church, or "church clothes." We were standing in a long line of people. I remember my brother and myself being angrily marched to the front row of the church. We were left to sit there quietly while strangers were crying. We were at our dad's funeral. I was eight years old.

On into my adulthood, I longed for love. My daddy's love.

Every summer, my mom would let us stay with our maternal grandmother so we could spend time with our cousins. I laugh now, but every time I would see my grandmother, who we called "Big Momma," she would always tell me, "Don't have a fast tail; save yourself." She would be reminding me to remain a virgin until I got married. We would have so much fun and freedom at her house! We spent mornings walking back and forth across town in Union City, Tennessee. It seemed so big. We would get candy from Ms. Sarah's Candy House, play arcade games at the Fun-A-Thon, buy Jungle Juice from the corner gas station, and flirt with the boys at the Boys & Girls Club. This felt like the best life. As I got older, I realized that

I loved to receive attention from the boys. I wanted to dress a certain way and look a certain way to get their attention. I was getting their attention, but I didn't realize it was leading to the wrong attention from high school boys as well as grown men. I believe this wrong attention led to me being molested by a family member, and I allowed it. I could've screamed, because there were other people sleeping in the house, but I didn't. While it was happening, I felt a strong hit on my back. When I turned to look, it was my aunt whupping me and the family member at the same time. I remember going to my grandmother's house the next day. I had welts all over my arms, back, and legs. It was summer, and all I had to wear were shorts and tank tops. I remember one of my aunts saying, "Glenda is going to kill her for beating that girl like that." I didn't even tell my mother what had happened. I don't even know if anyone else told her either. It didn't matter to me because I blamed myself. I told myself it was my fault, and I had gotten what I deserved. I felt disgusted and dirty. I didn't want the attention anymore, not like that.

My mom returned to pick us up from our summer break, and there was a man who we didn't know driving the car. My mom said that he was her husband and that they had gotten married. My brother asked him if we could call him Daddy. He turned to us and said, "Yeah, you can call me Daddy." He was good to us but very strict. He made us mean like the bulldogs he was breeding. We had to learn how to shoot guns. We were punished if our aim was off too many times when doing rounds. If he saw us fighting with someone in the yard, and it looked as if we had lost the fight, we were beaten and had to go back outside to start the fight again. We weren't allowed to go outside if they weren't home. The only place we could eat and have food was in the kitchen. It was mandatory that we cleaned the entire house every Saturday. We didn't do a lot of traveling, but he did allow us to continue visiting our relatives in Tennessee during the summer.

One summer, my grandmother remarried. While visiting her new home, I went in to get a drink of water, and a man followed me to the kitchen. He rubbed my butt, and when I turned to walk away, he grabbed me and pulled me to him, groping and rubbing my breast. I was confused, but I also felt fear and hate. My mom had told me and my brother that if anyone ever touched us inappropriately, we shouldn't be afraid to tell someone. I was too afraid to tell anyone about what happened to me that day, but I was determined to tell if anything like that happened again.

Summer was over, and a new year had begun at school. I was excited to be in middle school. In my mind, this was a big school, and it had everything. In the school gym, there were snacks for sale at recess. There were these rainbow-powdered-texture suckers that I loved. The price was twenty-five cents. Sometimes I would have a quarter; sometimes I wouldn't. One day, I noticed my stepfather putting change in a jar under his bed. Every morning, after he would leave for work, I would go into their room and get a quarter out of the jar. It went from a quarter a day to two quarters a day. I eventually lost count. I noticed that the jar was getting low, but I kept getting into it. One morning, I didn't know he was still in the house. I went into the room, and he said, "What is it?" He startled me, so I replied, "I need money for the concession stand." He was lying in bed. He didn't have a shirt on. He told me to get the jar and hand it to him. As I was handing it to him, he grabbed my arm, pulled me close to the bed, and said, "What are you willing to do for it?" Oh, my goodness, not again! Not from the man I call "Daddy!" I got out of there so fast. All I remember saying was, "The bus is coming." He replied, "I'm going to whup you if you tell somebody." This shook my world. That school day was a blank. I was going to tell somebody. I didn't want it to happen again. I had seven teachers that day. I didn't feel comfortable telling any of them. When I got home, I patiently waited for my mom to get home. I was going to tell. I had to tell. When she arrived, I just blurted it out. "Daddy tried to touch me." She had a blank stare. She had me tell her everything that happened. I can't even remember what she said, but I knew she was going to confront him. I felt relieved. I went to bed feeling nervous about telling her. A few days passed, and Mom hadn't mentioned anything to me about what I told her. One night, she had to work overtime, so it was just my brother and me at home. Daddy came into the house, and he told my brother to go outside and mow the yard. It was dark outside. He then told me to wash the dishes. He stood over me the whole time I was washing dishes. I was nervous and furious at the same time. I wasn't going to allow this to happen to me again. I rinsed the first set of dishes, and he said, "You're not rinsing them right. Soap suds are still on them." I rinsed the second set, and he began to hit me with a belt repeatedly. I instantly knew it was because I had told. He was angry! I don't know how long he whupped me, but I was bleeding afterward. He told me to go get in the tub. I was so afraid to undress and even more afraid to put water and soap on the open cuts. I don't know if it was paranoia or real, but while I was in the tub, I felt like he was watching me through the crack in the door.

Why was this happening to me? If my mom had confronted him, why were we still here? Wait, maybe she didn't believe me? How long would I have to go through this? For years, I carried with me the hurt that my mom believed him over me. The feeling of not being able to have a real dad was unbearable. I trusted no one. I began to hate everyone, including myself.

CHAPTER 2
WRONG KIND OF LOVE

It was an ordinary day. My brother and I had made it home from school. Mom was packing when we walked in. She told us to help her pack because we were moving. I went into the kitchen to help. She told us to leave two of everything: two forks, spoons, knives, plates…two of everything. This was a very disciplined household. We knew not to ask questions, only to obey. I wondered why we were leaving. What would we do? Where would we go? What did Daddy do to make her leave? She did not believe me when I told her what he did. What changed?

We moved into a trailer park in another city. We were allowed to continue our education at the school we were currently in because it was the middle of the school year. At this time, I was in middle school. The high school boys were catching my eye. I wanted a boyfriend. I wanted to receive gifts and balloons at school and have someone to carry my books while walking me to class, holding my hand, and kissing me. I wanted a kiss badly. I still longed for attention.

One day, one of the guys in high school began to show me some attention. We began to talk every day. The giggles and conversation were nonstop. My heart would flutter, seeing him from a distance in the hallway. He finally asked me to be his girlfriend. Without hesitation, I accepted, but there was one problem: my mom had a house rule; I had to be eighteen before I could have a boyfriend. I was only fifteen at the time. For a while, we just hid the relationship from everyone. One day, my mom and I were talking. I asked her about the rule of being eighteen before I could date. She was still dead set on keeping that rule. I told her about the young man that was interested in me. I asked her if she would meet with him and his mother. She would see for herself that they were good people. After weeks of me pestering her, she finally agreed.

He was the perfect gentleman when we arrived at his home. His mom and my mom talked. They gave us rules that they were expecting us to follow without rebuttal. At that point, I would have agreed to anything that they required. I just wanted a boyfriend. I felt that now that I finally had my first boyfriend, I would feel better about myself, even pretty. I wrote about him in my diary every night, how cute he was and how I loved it when he would hold my hand. I loved him, and he loved me. Time passed, and our attraction was growing past just holding hands and kissing. I would dream of more. I wanted more. When we were at school, it was rare that I would see him, because of the grade gap, but when I did, the butterflies in my stomach would be deep and heavy. One of my guy cousins would always tell me that he was too old for me, but I didn't care. I wanted what I wanted, and I was in love.

One particular night, I was allowed to go to a basketball game. I was excited to get dressed up and go to the game. I was excited, and I felt cute. When I arrived at the game, I went to my usual seat in the stands, near the student section, with my friends. We had our usual singing and chanting battle with the opposing team's student section across the court.

After the game, I waited outside for him to come out. I got in the car with him. He told me he wanted to take me somewhere before taking me home. He turned down a dirt road that was a path in a field. He drove until he found an opening where he could park. We talked for a moment and began to kiss. He laid my seat back and pulled me closer. We begin to kiss again. He proceeded to pull my panties down and get on top of me. I could feel him trying to unbutton his pants, but at that moment, I was hearing my Big Momma say, "Are you still a virgin?" I begin to say, "I can't," but he was still tugging at his pants, but quicker. "No, I can't." Then I said his name loudly. "*I can't do this.*" He paused for a brief second and proceeded anyway. I just remember lying there, being as still as I could. Numb. I did this. I had heard guys talking about girls leading guys on. I told myself, "This is your fault, Aimee." I was no longer a virgin. I felt disappointed and knew that my grandmother would be disappointed in me too.

I tried my best to dodge him at school, and he knew it. I was not doing my regular route or routine. During what we called "recess," the freshmen and upperclassmen would break at the same time, but in separate locations, except for the concession stand. We all had to go to the same stand. My friend group was pretty big. About four girls and five guys. I told them that I had broken up with him, and I wasn't talking to him again. While I was at the concession stand, he approached me. I walked away, but he followed me. He kept calling my name while following me. I was trying to get back to my group quickly. As I approached my group of friends, he grabbed my arm tightly and pulled me to him, and in the blink of an eye, my guy friends grabbed him and put him up against the wall. I heard one of them yelling, "You better not ever grab her like that again. She said she doesn't want to talk to you, so don't talk to her." I looked back, and they had him by the front collar of his shirt up against the wall, and two of the other guys had each of his arms pinned.

Later that day, the bell to switch classes rang. I was leaving one building and heading to another one, and there he was, waiting on me. Why wouldn't he just leave me alone? He grabbed me by both arms again, this time looking at me and saying, "Are you OK?" I replied, "I'm fine," but I wasn't. What could I say? We just stood there looking at each other for a brief second. I was so cold toward him. I felt nothing. Empty. He let me go. I went on into the building.

The bus I rode home would pass his house every day. One day, a group of boys were in his yard, laughing and pointing as we passed by. I cried a little during that ride home because I felt he had told all of them he had scored. I went from disgust to sobbing. From sobbing to feeling nothing. From feeling nothing to anger, and from anger to hate. It all just happened quickly.

CHAPTER 3
CHANGES

It's a new year, and my mom has been informed that we would have to attend the school in our district. I was going to be the new kid, and I wanted to impress everyone. I wanted to see myself differently. I wanted to be liked even though I was so unsure of myself. I was gaining friends. I was good at a lot of things. I loved ag class, welding, and mixing clay, heating it and making ceramics. I also enjoyed making birdhouses and paddles out of wood, researching on computers, and learning how to work and operate the floppy disks. I also liked to sing, dance, and watch *In Living Color*. I was the female version of Homey the Clown. I walked around with a stuffed sock, hitting classmates on the head with it if they said something stupid. I was bringing attention to myself.

One day, we had class elections for "most likely to succeed" in different areas in life. I was nominated for a couple of things. My name was called over the intercom with those of the other candidates. I remember changing classes, and a few of my friends were excited for me. Even I was excited. As we stood in line, waiting for a class to be dismissed, I heard a voice say, "Most likely to succeed as a ho, Aimee Triplet." I looked up, and two girls were giggling, and one girl in the middle was just looking at me with a smirk. I went on to class like nothing had even happened. When I came out of class, she said it again. When I went to the cafeteria, she said it again. Playground, again. Everywhere I went, she would find me and repeat the same thing: "Most likely to succeed as a ho, Aimee Triplet." This went on for days. It eventually changed to her just calling me a ho everyday.

Momma noticed a change in my behavior, and she began to question me about what was going on. I told her I had three bullies, but I didn't want to be fighting. In my mind, I wanted to be different. I remember my mom coming home one day and saying, "I talked to one of the girls' mother, and she thought it was funny that they were bullying you. I want you to grab the biggest one of them and tear into her." I wanted to be different so badly. I had made up my mind that I was not going to be fighting. That's what I had been known for at the other school. Trying to be grown, trying to be the big and bad girl, and look where it got me. No, I wanted to be different. I wanted to be somebody else. I began to ignore and dodge. I took different routes, waited to the end to leave for another class or left early to wait in the bathroom before class began. I remember seeing the one who would always call me a ho. She was taunting a guy on the playground. She just kept pushing, hitting, and taunting him. He finally turned around and jabbed her in the face about four or five times. I don't think she messed with anyone on the playground again.

A few months had passed, and my stepfather had started coming over to our new home. Things were going pretty well, but I just didn't feel comfortable around him anymore. I didn't trust him. I was just a kid. I felt like my mom must've loved him more than me because she didn't believe me when I told her what had happened. My trust level was a little to none. One day, I arrived home earlier than usual, and his van was parked between our trailer and the one facing our front door. I went into our trailer, and he wasn't inside. I went to grab a snack, and I heard a squeaking sound, but I didn't think anything of it. I heard it again. It was coming from outside. I looked out of the front-room window, and his van was rocking. I went outside to check. I pulled the van door back, and he was naked with a woman on top of him. He looked me dead in my eyes, and I just pulled the door shut as hard as I could. I turned my back to walk away, and the van started rocking again. In my mind, Momma ain't gone believe me, so why even say anything? They eventually got a divorce, but the damage—the seeds of distrust, being disloyal, manipulative, and hateful—had already been planted. I hated my life, and I didn't care who knew it. Mask off! I became ruthless and reckless. I was dating guys and girls. I wasn't committing to anyone. If I had any feelings for anyone I was dating, or if they had feelings for me, I would end the relationship and discontinue all contact immediately. Technology wasn't like it is now, so it was easy to do.

I was living my life. I found myself hanging out with my guy friends and maybe two to three girls that weren't afraid to ride out to parties and hangout spots with me. I had about four different friend groups. One set was from my grade school. These were the guys that were always ready to throw down and get into whatever. They would say, "If anyone ever messes with you, just tell us; this place will be surrounded in less than five minutes, with nowhere to run." Another set was five girls who loved to sing and laugh. They would attend parties with me. There was never a dull moment with them. There was one close girlfriend who was always honest with me but would still get out there with me in my wrong. My ride or die. We were friends for years, to the point that no matter how much time passed, we always picked right back up where we left off. Then there was my best man. I could just relax and not think about anything. He was like a heaven-sent counselor. He never upheld my wrong or pitied me. I would even try to get him to do some devious stuff, and he never detoured or wavered. He was a true example of friendship and goodness.

One thing I wish I had courage to do while I was in my youth was to apologize for the hurt and discomfort I caused for so many people because of my inward hurt. I became an angry bully. I taunted and humiliated people. Pulled guns and knives on people. Ran over a guy with my car. Had girls jumped. Despicable and devilish things that stemmed from me always desiring to have a father that I felt would never be in my reach. My pain, hurt, and disgust led to me whoring after attention and fake love. I was young when I accepted Christ into my life, but there was always something inside of me that wanted to be desired and fulfilled. The church wasn't satisfying my desires. At a certain point in my life, I didn't think anything would.

We were under the Pentecostal belief. I remember wanting to wear pants because I wanted to play basketball and softball. I was good at it, but I would have to wear a skirt. There were always so many rules that seemed to be only for women. I couldn't wear pants, makeup, or nail polish, but I could wear miniskirts. I couldn't cut my hair or even go to the movie theater. If I did any of these things, I was going to hell. There seemed to be more focus on what I couldn't do and nothing that I could do. I begged my mom every day about wearing pants, and her answer would always be no. I started borrowing leggings and changing into them at school. The ministry we were in would always put me in Bible trivia competitions with other ministries' youth departments. I was good at that too. I liked to win, and I liked it when I made our leader feel proud. While studying and reading, I read that a woman shouldn't wear anything pertaining to a man. I had heard that verse multiple times, but this time, I studied for myself. We didn't have quick access to the internet during that time, so I had to pull out my encyclopedias. In the pictures, it looked like all the women and men wore robe-like garments. I told my mom what I had found, and she replied that when I got a job, I could buy my own clothes. As long as she was buying them, she would not purchase any pants.

My mom's friend was a manager at a restaurant in the mall. Because of my mom, she hired me. I was so excited. What's the first thing you think I did with my first check? You're right! I paid my tithes and purchased a pair of pants. They were purple jeans that I know I probably wore every day until I purchased more. I can't say it was the happiest day of my life, but I was very happy. I was able to make a decision for myself. It felt liberating. Of course then I felt like I was grown.

I was called into a church meeting with our leader at the time, his wife, and my mother. It was about the pants. As he explained the scripture Deuteronomy 22:5, I listened. Even as I write this, I still see myself standing, while they were sitting. I went in with a chip on my shoulder. I knew it was about the pants when I arrived. Out of respect, I wore a dress to the meeting, but I was ready to debate, with my not-so-grown self. I told him what I had found and that everyone wore clothing that looked like robes or gowns. He stressed that there was a difference between the men's and women's clothing. In my mind, there wasn't. He finally asked me if I was going to continue wearing pants. I responded, "Yes sir." His wife looked at me with so much disappointment and told me that I was going to hell if I continued to wear the pants. I responded, "Well I'm going first-class." Looking back, saying that was very disrespectful. I spoke at a conference, and this memory came to mind while speaking, and at that very moment, I wished I had taken an opportunity to apologize to them. They were my first pastors, and I learned so much from them both. I learned how to study the word for myself, how to dress with modesty, how to sow willingly, how to practice choir etiquette and fellowship, and how to stand on what I believed. As a child, it all looked bad. As an adult, I see it was for my good. That "first-class" comment set me on a path to self-destruction.

By the time my senior year of high school arrived, I was going to school in the daytime and working at a factory at night because I had been fired from the job my mom's friend had hired me for. She said it was for missing a day of work, but deep down, I knew it was because I had been stealing money and giving away free food. Just like any teen today, I was angry and upset with her even though I was the one in the wrong. I needed that job so I could graduate. It was a part of my academic schedule to have a job throughout the last semester of classes. My mom got me on at the local factory so I would graduate.

I was so out of control that my senior class shirt read, "6 Million Ways To Die, Choose One." I was not afraid of dying, and if necessary, I wasn't afraid to kill. It would be death by self-destruction. I went on this emotional wave for at least two years before recommitting to God in another ministry. This ministry literally halted the destructive spirit that was looming over my life.

CHAPTER 4
BONDED & FREE

I was nineteen when he proposed to me. I was establishing a routine of not only attending church but also working in the church. I was still employed at the local factory when I met him. There were so many people against our relationship, but I had fallen in love. I mean, he worked, had his own life, and believed in Christ. He faithfully went to church with me, and he understood the scriptures.

We were having a wonderful time together. We even worked together in numerous departments in the church. Things were going so well. One night, when he was dropping me off at home, he gave me a serious look and said, "I have to tell you something." I remember my heart beginning to pound. I thought to myself, "Please don't let it be what everyone has been telling me about him being in the closet." He looked at me and said, "I'm married. We're separated, and I'm working on getting a divorce." I begin to ask so many questions. I couldn't understand why he hadn't told me this when he told me he had a child. At this time in my life, I didn't understand the true concept of love. I only understood the visual and hearing portions of love that were displayed on TV and through music. I had a grasp of "entertainment love." I felt like we could get through it if he would show me his divorce papers when it was final.

We were doing what married couples do. We had a joint banking account. I had given him my car to drive because his was broken down. I was cooking for him, preparing meals, taking trips with him, and spending time with his child. I was committed, but something began to change. He began to grow distant. We began to argue a lot. All of my childhood trauma would explode on him during those arguments. I would cuss him, hit him, and degrade him with cruel words every time we argued. We attended a Fourth of July revival together. The speaker made a comment, saying, "Young ladies, stop letting these young men use your body; when they are done with you, they will move on to the next one." That pierced my heart. I wouldn't have been so angry if I hadn't become so vulnerable to him. That night, I told him that I didn't want to have sex again until we were married. He agreed.

A few weeks passed, and I found out that he was in another relationship with a young lady who was related to my stepfather. I had been seeing her at different events and services, but I didn't think anything of it until it was brought to my attention. It was true, and it hurt. Not because it ended, but because I had allowed him to overpower the relationships that I had with my family and friends. I had cut them all from my life because they couldn't trust him. My mom would always say, "It's just something about him that I can't put my finger on. Be careful." After the breakup, I was called into a young adult group meeting, not knowing that the meeting was about the breakup. I felt humiliated already; why were we having a meeting about it? The young lady who had told me he was cheating was scolded for telling me. The question asked to the group in the meeting was "What if Aimee had brought a gun in here and started shooting?" I was stunned! Was my past life the reason for the meeting? Were people frightened of me? I thought I was forgiven. I thought old things were passed away, and all things were made new. I felt like I was an adult at the time. I wanted to leave the church, but I truly did love God more than I loved hating myself. When I longed for my biological father, God became my father just from me asking Him, "God, will you be my father?" The visions and dreams He would show me as a child were outstanding, and I wanted that back. I wanted God more than the feeling of humiliation, so I stayed, and I served, and served, and served. Whatever was asked of me, I did. I didn't even realize that I was still whoring. Whoring after attention, accolades, and recognition. Whoring after the act of trying to convince people that I had changed. That I wasn't the violent bully they had heard about. There were two of me, one bonded, one free. It felt good. It felt normal, but it wasn't God.

CHAPTER 5
WHORING FOR FREE

When this title came to me, I instantly thought, "My goodness, people are going to think that I'm calling myself a whore." In actuality, I am. The things I did and the sins I committed were actions of whoredom. Everything I did, I was doing it for something in return, attention and/or validation. Think about Hosea, the man who God told to marry a harlot. It didn't matter what he did, thought, or prayed; nothing ever satisfied his wife. She was a woman of the streets, or as some say, "the world," and that's where her desires were, in the streets. "So as a man thinketh, so is he." The world was her, and she was the world. She had steak and craved slop. She had the finest silks and desired rags. She had the finest and purest water and desired to dip from a toilet. As Hosea 4:12 (New International Version) states, "My people inquire of a piece of wood, and their walking staff gives them oracles. For a spirit of whoredom has led them astray, and they have left their God to play the whore."

I had left God when I was a teenager. My childhood trauma wasn't my choice, but when Jesus was presented to me, it was my choice to decide whether I would stay in my filth or allow the Holy Spirit to guide me and direct me.

I was so excited about this title that I began to tell those who were close to me. I even had someone to ask me, "So what made Jeremy marry you, knowing you had been with a lot of men?" I replied, "I never said I had been with a lot of men." My cravings and desires made me a whore. I knew by assumption that a large percentage of people were going to think that this book would be referring to the act of sex for pay, but it's not about the act of sex; it's the act of whoring. It's defined as not only prostitution but also faithless, unworthy, idolatrous practices or pursuits. We see it every day. Men and women prefer to befriend their children instead of being their father or mother because the desire or idolatrous pursuit to be liked by our children and their friends is more important than training a child in the way he or she should go, not only in the Lord, but in life. Now we have a generation of senior citizens catering to the grown children that they birthed by raising their grandchildren out of guilt and resentment. Children are happy, dedicated, and secure in playing sports but are angry, uncomfortable, and insecure to be a part of the local youth ministries, and parents allow it. We prefer to rest, wash cars, and eat big meals on Sunday, rather than staying fifteen minutes later than usual to witness to a lost soul in Morning Manna. We can be in the building already and still refuse to extend our clocks, arms, and understanding to the lost. We say stuff like "We are the church" and, in the same breath, put God on a time limit. The sad part about this is that we, in turn, will stay for double overtime at a basketball, soccer, or football game and won't complain. I'm grateful that God married us anyway! He proclaimed His love for us with the ultimate sacrifice, Jesus. Yet we prefer to continue to choose the paganistic and unholy ways of the world. Rahab was recorded as a whore but risked her life to save others. That counted for something. Jesus became part of her lineage. Greatness was in her blood.

I could see greatness in me, but I couldn't accept that it was actually in me. My doubt overpowered my will to care. I craved an open word from God in front of people, because if they could hear it too, they would see it and treat me as such: great. It didn't always happen. This would leave me feeling unseen or unappreciated. One day, I decided to stop looking for validation and appreciate who I was and who God was creating me to be. I also had to walk in what he called me to be, an image of him, love. I had to begin by loving myself and not responding from my emotions or from what I couldn't control. If you're reading this, you can do the same. Remind yourself to kill your fleshly desires. Make it submissive to the hand of God. Do not sell yourself for cheap. Reading the book of Hosea makes me constantly ask the question, "What happened to his wife as a child that made her desire the opposite of what God had given her?" He gave her a man who loved her unconditionally, and deep down, she still felt unworthy. Have you ever felt unworthy, undeserving? Have thoughts ever run across your mind reminding you of the wrong you have done? Does it keep you from moving forward? You have to train your mind and remind yourself that you are somebody, and you are forgiven. All have sinned and come short of His glory. Whose glory? God's glory. I look at it like this: everyone has a work to do within themselves. The work begins in our minds.

CHAPTER 6
RENT-FREE

Who's controlling your mind? Who are you allowing to live in your head rent-free? If you find yourself missing a family gathering because of certain family members you don't want to see, their rent is free. If you leave a job because of this one person who you just couldn't get along with, their rent is free. If you stop attending a ministry because the one you loved broke your heart, and he or she is still there, their rent is free. If you stay in your car for a few extra minutes so you don't have to walk by or near someone that irritates you, their rent is free. You have given that person a valuable piece of you, power. They are controlling you without even saying a word to you. I call that psychic power. I allowed all the trauma of my childhood to weigh in my head for way longer than I should have, and it all stemmed from my "daddy issues." It became my crutch to make excuses for every foul thing I did. My feelings of neglect, insecurity, anger, and attention had to be dealt with before I ruined myself, my marriage, and my children's lives.

I often asked myself, "How can a man that's not even alive have so much power or control over my emotional state? How can a tenant stay in an apartment complex rent-free?" The owner has to allow it. The circumstances and the question of why aren't even factors. The key to rent-free is allowance. Allowance is defined as the amount of something that is permitted, especially within a set of regulations or for a specified purpose. Wow! Allowance is something that is permitted, and the purpose was unaware self-destruction. I gave my issues permission to stay rent-free. I put all my resources, energy, and time into wanting to feel love. I wanted that Eros love and that Ludus love discussed by Elizabeth Rider. I never even considered that all I needed was self-love. I was in it, and I couldn't even see my issues. I was blinded by me. This caused me to seek for something I would never have, my dad. Even when he was alive, he had his own wife and children. My brother and I weren't part of that. I could never wrap my head around that because I still wanted what I wanted, my dad. In the Book of Hosea, his wife, Gomer, wanted what she wanted. The lustful desire was in her. It was a part of her. She was in it. Her spirit and her adulterous spirit had become one. When you find yourself sitting alone, wondering, "Who am I?" because of things you've done or said, it may be because the issue(s) you deal with are just dealing with you. It's controlling you. It's becoming one with you. After I pinpointed that my issues derived from my childhood daddy issues, the actions I took after I came to this realization were on me. I've never liked the blame game, so I had and have no one to blame but me. How could I evict something that had become a part of me? It was me, and I was it. I disconnected from the church. I just completely stopped working in the church. I knew I didn't want to bleed my inward sins over into people. I called a friend and told her, "I'm quitting everything. Church, motherhood, marriage, school, everything." I was done. Honestly, I was tired. I was tired of me. She said, "How are you going to quit something that's not going to quit you? God is with you, always; he's not quitting you. You can't quit." That day, we began a motivational game. We had to think on the things that were true, honest, just, pure, lovely, and of good report, then send texts throughout the day with one word of motivation. The only rule was to take turns. This made us focus in on the goodness of God all day. Nothing negative. I remember going a whole day without thinking about all the wrong I had done. Then another day passed, and another, and another. We were having streaks without even knowing what streaks were. I'm appreciative of that time in my life.

Philippians 4:8 has been my go-to scripture when insecurities and doubt try to rise back up inside of me. This is why, when I speak, I speak about myself and God. When I teach, I aim to motivate and encourage by reminding people to kill this flesh and make it submissive to the hand of God. My life is a living example of dos and do nots. You will never be able to be honest with others until you're honest with yourself. Your issue(s) may be similar to mine, the same as mine, or even totally different. Whatever they are, address them. Address you! Strive to be better, and surround yourself with people who will not only hold you accountable but also encourage you.

CHAPTER 7
ATTENTION-GETTERS VS. ATTENTION-RECEIVERS

When I think of attention-getters, they are the ones who are getting all the attention at the current time. Attention-receivers are the ones who are receiving attention. Attention-getters are going out and doing whatever they can do to get attention with no worries about the backlash or consequences.

Take a child that feels like their parent or parents don't pay them any attention. They are about to do whatever it takes to get their attention. They might break stuff, make embarrassing remarks in a crowded room, steal the car, wreck it, get in trouble with the law, get suspended from school, etc.... An adult might change their wardrobe, hairstyle, or Facebook status, dress more provocatively, flirt more, anything it takes to get their Facebook follower numbers up.

Attention-receivers aren't trying to receive any attention, but their good deeds are constant, and eventually, someone decides to thank them publicly. Someone in the crowd realizes that the attention-receiver did a similar thing for them so they decide to give a public thanks as well. Then there's a ripple effect in which multiple people begin to give thanks to the attention-receiver. They are unselfish givers; therefore, the gift returns to them.

The attention-getters take. That's why they always feel like something has been taken from them or they are not getting what they feel they deserve. They always want more. I always wanted more, never satisfied. Even when I thought I didn't, I did. When I began to see myself, things changed. It's something when you ask God to open your eyes. Ha, and you think he's going to show you other people, but he shows you *you*. I was an attention-getter. Have you ever been in a meeting about one thing, and the meeting ends up being about the person in the room who made the meeting completely about them? You have a whole agenda in front of you, and someone, the attention-getter, has their own personal agenda lined up. When God showed me myself, it didn't feel good. We are so quick to say, "I'm not perfect. No one is," but we walk around high-minded, like we know everything, when in actuality, we don't even know ourselves.

There are all types of attention-getters. I mentioned the one who detours the meeting toward themself, but let's talk about the one who walks into the meeting like they are mad at the world. One by one, people begin to ask them, "Are you OK?" The most noticeable response is "I don't like coming to these meetings." In my mind, I'm asking the question, "Why are they even here?" They don't even realize that they are the one who brought the spirit of confusion and conflict into the meeting. Ha! Attention-getter!

Attention-getters come in all types of positions and titles. Ask yourself, "Am I an attention-getter or receiver?" Are you taking what you think belongs to you, or are you receiving the honor and respect given freely to you? Getters say things like, "After all I've done for you or them! That should've been mine! She doesn't deserve that! I'm the one who came up with that idea! Look what I did! I did that first! They like them more than they like me! They can't get with me because I'm real!" Real what? Because you really can't even see yourself, Aimee! But what do you do when you can't see yourself? Again, ask God to show you *you*. No one else. You. In the book of John 3:1–18 from *The Message* Bible, it reads, "There was a man of the Pharisee sect, Nicodemus, a prominent leader among the Jews. Late one night he visited Jesus and said, 'Rabbi, we all know you're a teacher straight from God. No one could do all the God-pointing, God-revealing acts you do if God weren't in on it.'" Jesus said, "You're absolutely right. Take it from me: Unless a person is born from above, it's not possible to see what I'm pointing to—to God's kingdom." "How can anyone," said Nicodemus, "be born who has already been born and grown up? You can't reenter your mother's womb and be born again. What are you saying with this 'born-from-above' talk?"

Jesus said, "You're not listening. Let me say it again. Unless a person submits to this original creation—the 'wind-hovering-over-the-water' creation, the invisible moving the visible, a baptism into a new life—it's not possible to enter God's kingdom. When you look at a baby, it's just that: a body you can look at and touch. But the person who takes shape within is formed by something you can't see and touch—the Spirit—and becomes a living spirit. So don't be so surprised when I tell you that you have to be 'born from above'—out of this world, so to speak. You know well enough how the wind blows this way and that. You hear it rustling through the trees, but you have no idea where it comes from or where it's headed next. That's the way it is with everyone 'born from above' by the wind of God, the Spirit of God." Nicodemus asked, "What do you mean by this? How does this happen?" Jesus said, "You're a respected teacher of Israel and you don't know these basics? Listen carefully. I'm speaking sober truth to you. I speak only of what I know by experience; I give witness only to what I have seen with my own eyes. There is nothing secondhand here, no hearsay. Yet instead of facing the evidence and accepting it, you procrastinate with questions. If I tell you things that are plain as the hand before your face and you don't believe me, what use is there in telling you of things you can't see, the things of God? No one has ever gone up into the presence of God except the One who came down from that Presence, the Son of Man. In the same way that Moses lifted the serpent in the desert so people could have something to see and then believe, it is necessary for the Son of Man to be lifted up and everyone who looks up to him, trusting and expectant, will gain a real life, eternal life. This is how much God loved the world: He gave his Son, his one and only Son. And this is why: so that no one need be destroyed; by believing in him, anyone can have a whole and lasting life. God didn't go to all the trouble of sending his Son merely to point an accusing finger, telling the world how bad it was. He came to help, to put the world right again. Anyone who trusts in him is acquitted; anyone who refuses to trust him has long since been under the death sentence without knowing it. And why? Because of that person's failure to believe in the one-of-a-kind Son of God when introduced to him."

I had put myself under a death sentence. Even after I felt I had done my time, I still put myself back behind bars. Back behind the bars of wanting attention. I had to be born again. I had given my life to God. Then I backslid. I rededicated my life to him and backslid again, in the church. This passage of scripture was in an online lesson dealing with Nicodemus asking Jesus a question that he felt, by human knowledge and theory, would be impossible to answer. How could a man possibly be born again when he is an adult? First, the man he speaks of is definitely himself. Second, he desired the change, but his eyes had to be open to see himself. "Open my eyes so I can see what you show me of your miracle wonders" (Psalms 119:18). When your eyes are open, you will definitely see yourself as well. It caused me to look inward first, and then outward. I went from seeking attention to spreading the message of love. Loving God, loving people, and loving myself. I placed a slogan in my heart, "Love Always Wins." I felt rejuvenated and at peace. Then came more trials and tribulations.

CHAPTER 8
SUICIDAL THOUGHTS

During my childhood, I had a lot of suicidal thoughts. It wasn't something that was talked about in our community or home. You weren't given any brochures or helpline counseling numbers to speak with someone to privately help you through your feelings. All I really remember is the commercial with the egg and frying pan demonstrating, "This is your brain on drugs." I would see that commercial and think to myself that I was the egg being fried by life. I masked it, though. People may have seen a lot of things, but I'm sure no one saw the suicidal spirit. My senior shirt screamed "suicide." It read, "6 Million Ways To Die, Choose 1." No one ever took the time to ask me questions. I believe no one knew how to because it was not talked about in the black communities. I remember being on a date, and the young man said something that I didn't like, and I swerved the steering wheel back and forth in the middle of the road while driving on a back road. I didn't care if we lived or died. I slammed on the brakes because I could see the fear in his eyes. When the car stopped, he jumped out of the car and began to walk in the opposite direction. I drove off. We never spoke again. When I rededicated my life, Elder Mary J. Parks took my hand and stood by me in front of the congregation. I felt a freshness. Because of the Pentecostal teachings that I had previously been under, it was easy for me to just stop doing what that movement had taught me was sin. I didn't stop wearing my pants, though. I just wouldn't wear them to church. There was one time when my mom was at the headquarters church, preparing a lunch for the congregation, and she asked me to bring her something that she needed for one of the meals. I told her OK, but she would have to come out and get it because I had on pants. Of course, when I arrived, she couldn't come out, and I had to go in. My goodness, I thought everyone in there was whispering and talking about me. It was an overload of uncomfortable! I'm surprised I didn't faint. I knew how to calm myself with the techniques I had learned after experiencing an anxiety attack the year before. I didn't have a clue that the anxiety was tied to my depression. I wish someone had known. I wish someone could have seen my struggle.

Now that I've experienced it and have lived through it, it's easy for me to ask someone, "Are you OK," or "Are you good?" I know it's improper, but you have to know how to communicate with all people.

Depression will have you sitting in dark rooms and places, thinking about all the wrong you have done and who you did it to or with. It will make you feel like no one cares about you or your existence. It will block your mind from the ones who love you the most. The ones that genuinely care for you. It will make you think that you have no real friends. If you were a character in a movie, it would make you see yourself as the villain. You will find yourself sick a lot. I would stop eating meals and still gained weight because when I ate, it would be whole pies or whole bags of cookies. When you do go out in the public, it's either a rehearsed smile, fake interest in things, or moments when people are hating to be around you because you always have negative thoughts or comments. Yeah, you look happy on the outside, but the real you is in the inside, and nine times out of ten, what's on the inside is definitely going to show itself on the outside. A majority of this is shown through our words.

My depression was hidden well in public, but the ones closest to me received all the after-hours buildup. I always felt lonely or alone, even in a crowded room. Just uncomfortable. Around 2010 or 2011, I consulted my current watch-care pastor, Apostle Jessie Webb. I told him what was going on in my life. I told him that my life was like a roller coaster. It was going up and down, around a circle, then up and down again. He told me that I needed to pay attention to the seasons. To be aware of what season I was in, to reflect and think about what had happened during those seasons in my life. I narrowed it down to June, July, and August. These three months were the most depressing months for me. Not only depressing, but it seemed as if my finances would be limited to none during these months. Bills seemed to be higher, and there were a couple of times when there was more money going out the house than coming in. This increased my suicidal thoughts. I had to pray and get my mind right to focus on helping myself. I realized that June and July were the months we would visit our relatives in Tennessee. Something bad would always happen when we visited. This included the molestations. I was a stay-at-home mom, so the majority of my money came from my photography business. I looked at my calendar, and lot of my appointments for June, July, and August were small, like two or three appointments. Was I setting my appointments according to how I felt? Was I aiding in self-sabotage? I was allowing the enemy to use me to fight me. Active and working in ministry…dying. Going to Bible class and Sunday school every Wednesday and Sunday…dying. Do you know how it feels to be dead in the church? Thinking that nobody gets you. Nobody understands you. You don't even understand you. One moment you're up; then you're down. Bishop Clarence Parks would say, "Like an Almond Joy bar, sometimes you feel like a nut; sometimes you don't! Get up and let God free you and use you!" I pulled up all the courage and strength I had and told myself, "I will live, and not die, and declare the works of the Lord! Work, Lord!"

I'm feeling empowered in my spirit all over again just typing this! I speak this now in your life…depression, anxiety, and suicidal thoughts will not hold you captive or bonded. You will rise up and call yourself blessed because you are blessed going in and blessed coming out. You will come out of this. These demonic spirits of self-destruction will not hold you captive. Get up, and let God free you! Speak your freedom, walk in your freedom, and talk about your freedom! For the favor of the Lord is in your life and over your life. You will not be moved by what the enemy throws your way. You will walk in victory and assurance that your end *is* an expected end, and it shall be done in Jesus's name. Amen and amen.

CHAPTER 9
HIS THOUGHTS

On Thursday, January 12, 2023, I woke up, got out of bed, and stretched. I heard "thirty days" in my spirit. I heard it like a slight whisper. Something in me knew what it meant, because I immediately responded, "I can't do that." A quick run-through, like a fast-playing movie, played in my mind. There was so much stuff I had to do. There was no way I could disconnect for thirty days. I'm a guaranteed overthinker. Meaning that if there's anything I don't want to do or anything I think someone else isn't going to want me to do, it's guaranteed that I'm going to put too much time and focus on why I should or shouldn't do it. I tried my best to think about something else. I jumped on the elliptical. It usually clears my mind. Nope, didn't work. I had a scheduled Zoom call at 8:00 a.m.; surely this would help me to get the thirty days out of my head. I joined the call, and the host said, "I have a video I'm going to play. A lot of y'all need to hear this." The video began to play. "I know it's cold, but are you willing to step into uncharted territory? I need you to disappear for thirty days." Me: "Wait, what!" "I dare you to disconnect for thirty days." I took this as a direct, confirmed order from God. This could have meant various types of things. Trust and believe that I tried to make it be various types of things. After the Zoom call, I walked down to our washroom, and it was still in my spirit, but heavier. I asked God out loud, "What am I supposed to do?" His response was "book." I had been talking about this book for three years, telling anyone that would listen about this book that I hadn't even begun to write. I had reached out to my sister, Ebbennie, in 2021 with five book titles that I wanted her to create covers for. Even when I received them, I still didn't begin to write. This was different. I knew I was going to have to take a sabbatical and commune with God in order to get this all down on paper, but how was I going to take a sabbatical for thirty days with so much responsibility? I had just recently taken on a new job with Lack Must Leave Insurance Agency, and I was an administrator at Brooks Chapel Kingdom Harvest, a youth-lesson preparer for Sunday school, the owner of JH Printing and Photography, the Rawls Funeral Home program content and designer, UP Outreach & Resource Center's executive director, the director of One Soul at a Time Hybrid Women's Ministry, a marriage and women's counselor, a wife, and the mother of two community-active and -involved adults.

As I type this, I'm on day eight of my commune with God. I'm ahead according to the days but behind according to obedience. I told my husband the same day what God had placed in my spirit. Even with him, I tried to word it convincingly. In mid-sentence, he told me to do what God told me to do because he knows that I hear God. "But what about when I tell the people at the church? I don't want to hear all the 'You sure that was God? I think you need to pray about that. Maybe he was talking about something else, because God ain't gone tell you to miss church.'" My husband replied, "You really don't have to tell them anything. I'm saying, do what God told you to do. Don't worry about nothing else." I didn't want to be the latest conversation. The secular world always talks about canceling somebody, but it's nothing like when the church cancels you. That's another book for another time.

I called my mom. This was me still worrying because I was still looking for an opinion. I told her what God said, and she got really quiet. In the quietness, I said, "Exactly. This is exactly how church folks are going to be. I need to prepare myself for the backlash." She, too, eventually told me to do what God said to do, because the book needed to be completed. She asked me if I had talked to my pastor. I told her I was going to talk to him the next Friday while we were completing some things at the church.

Sidebar: We, the believers of Christ, are the church. The brick-and-mortar building that we go into is the place of worship. We are the church! When we grasp this, we can become the rock that God will build his church upon. Who will you hold up?

That following Friday, January 20, 2023, we arrived at the sanctuary a little before 10:00 a.m. I remember that my pastor wanted to show us what God had shown him. So my husband, the office clerk, and I went with him to the location God had shown him. After that, we headed back to the sanctuary, and there was a lot to be done, plus, we needed to prepare and make sure we had everything we needed for the next Fifth Sunday service.

Time passed quickly this particular day. I remember this only because we were to meet our children for an early dinner at 4:00 p.m. My husband stepped away for a second. When he reentered the sanctuary, I told our pastor what God had told me. At this point, I was tickled because he did the same thing my mom did: total quietness. I responded, "That's the same thing my mom did." He began to tell me his views on it. I remember getting so emotional and saying out loud, "I'm trying not to get emotional, but I know what God said, but the way I'm made up, I'm going to do what you say to do." He told me that God would tell me the reason why He wanted me to do it. I ensured him that the reason was for me to complete this book. He told me that if God said it, do what he says. But my overthinking, and now, the questioning, led me to doubt what God was saying to me.

On Monday, January 23, we had prayer at the church. One of our covenant pastors, Elder Lucille Hayes, visited that night. We were told to split into twos, confess, and pray for each other. She was sitting right behind me. I looked at her and said, "Has anyone texted or told you that they wanted you to be their partner? I want you to be my partner." No one had asked her, so we went to the hallway to pray. She told me that I had always relied on man's word, from my home place of worship to now. She stated that there would have to come a time when I obeyed God's word, because he speaks to me, but I always rely on man. She told me to hear God and do what he tells me to do. She also told me that even though I felt like procrastination was my issue, God said that it's not so much procrastination as it is prioritizing. Everything that's on my plate is not for me to do. Some things you have to scrape off your plate. She mimicked the motion with her hands. I'm a visual learner, and she gave me something to see. I didn't tell her what God had spoken in my spirit about the thirty days. I just hugged her and said "thank you." On Thursday, January 26, my pastor called to discuss upcoming events. As we talked, I slid in the thirty-days communion with God. It was just weighing too heavily in my spirit and in my heart. At the end of the discussion, he asked me when I would begin. I told him February 1 to March 2. Yeah, I had already looked up the dates because I was determined to obey God, and I wanted to make sure that anything that I had agreed to do would be completed.

I spoke on a topic, years ago, titled "It's Not What You See, But It's How You See It." I told my mom that I felt like I was being obedient and disobedient at the same time. It felt weird. I was supposed to have begun January 12, and I would have been done February 14. We know this date as Valentine's Day. I would be finishing on the day of love. That in itself was symbolic to me. Not saying that God cares anything about Valentine's Day. I'm saying that if I was looking for a sign, that was a sign, but I have never looked for signs…I look for approval. Whew! Approval stems from wanting attention. Mom said, "There's a story in the Bible about a man who had two sons. He asked them to do some work for him. One said that he wasn't going to do it. The other one said that he would do it. The one who said that he wasn't going to do it did the work. The one who said that he would do it didn't do the work. Which one do you think the father honored?" I replied, "He honored the one who did the work." She went on to say that it's not about when you started; it's about your obedience in starting. "You are doing what he told you to do. I know he's going to honor your obedience."

His thoughts toward me are of peace and not of evil. I have an expected end. I'm going to obey and run on to see what the end will be!

CHAPTER 10
FAITH NOT FEELINGS

I t's Friday, day ten of my journey with God. My mind is remembering what my mom said to me this week. "Aimee, you may not like what I'm about to say, but you have a hard time sticking to things. You must finish this book." She was right. I like to build things for people and move on. I've never cared for working for companies with a lot of rules. I've been an entrepreneur for over twenty-five years. I have just never charged what I was worth. This would lead me to have to get a secular job to bring extra money into the home. I worked multiple jobs part-time because I was the caregiver for my children. Now that they are adults, I can stick to something. It's definitely going to be something that I love to do and am not made to do. I've built my surroundings on faith, believing that God sees me, flaws and all.

Have I ever made any decisions based on my feelings? Yes, many times. I've made irrational decisions, impulsive decisions, and careless decisions. I had a hard time controlling my emotions. The quick impulse to yell, throw things, and scream were the moments that my emotions would control me. My husband and I have been married for twenty-four years. I know that in the first fifteen years of our marriage, I asked for a divorce more than twenty-four times. My happiness was like a sprint race, exciting at the starting gun, but in 12.4 seconds, it was over. Then I had to rebuild my confidence all over again. Shake off the doubt, the frustration, the worrying, the self-body-shaming, the hurt, the comparing, the self-hate, the self-mental-abuse, the overthinking, the helicopter thinking, and the warden mentality.

Yes, there's not one doubt that I have had a hard time sticking to things. I've known this my entire life. I had to make a conscious decision to check myself. I still have those "I'm leaving" thoughts. I trust God, and I have faith that he is still preparing a good work in me. I had to stop bottling things up and talk it out. I had to change my words because whether you believe it or not, they do have power. We have the power to set our own atmosphere. Our speech has to be faith-forward, not feelings-led.

I approached a majority of my days with how I felt. If I felt that today was a beautiful day, then it was going to be a beautiful day. If it was raining and cloudy, I would view it as a gloomy day, and you can't really do anything on a gloomy day if you're being controlled by your feelings.

My belief tells me that faith is the substance of things hoped for, the evidence of things not seen (Hebrews 11:1). The online dictionary states that it is complete trust in something or someone. Strong belief in God or in the doctrines of a religion, based on spiritual apprehension rather than proof.

In the early parts of my marriage, my husband and I were more dedicated to our church work (the building) than we were to our marriage (the actual church). The works of the church were our life. It was what we were doing before we got married, and it just carried over into the matrimony. There is nothing wrong with working in the ministry you are a part of, but never allow the work to become more important than the time you put into your spouse and children. There has to be a balance.

My husband and I were so dedicated to the ministry we were in that we were deemed Brother and Sister Faithful. It felt good, like an honor, even. We worked even harder, if not more. As time passed, it became a strain on our marriage, and the names Brother and Sister Faithful became more of an image to keep up than an honor. We were working hard in leadership roles in the building and fighting like children at home. I was the aggressor. I never felt like he loved me like he loved the church. I wasn't one who would submit if I did not feel like I was getting the attention I felt I deserved. My feelings always outweighed my faith. Looking back, I would even say stuff like, "I feel like we have enough to buy a house. I feel like we can get that. I feel like if we do this, we can do that," etc. To any married person reading this, always remember that when you're married, you two are becoming one. There's not a magical circumstance that automatically makes you one. You are two separate beings who are growing into one being. Most disagreements arise because in any argument, the ones arguing think or believe what they are saying is right. If we could just pause to really listen and comprehend each individual's views, the argument wouldn't last as long. I always felt like my husband didn't listen to me. I didn't realize that the way I was saying stuff was why he was turning a deaf ear. I was bossy, sarcastic, and mean. As individuals, none of us want to be treated that way. Over the past five years, we've been training ourselves to grow together, not individually. It hasn't always been easy, but it has been a learning experience.

Early during year six of our marriage, I heard the Lord say, "Move." I told my husband, and he told me that he hadn't heard the Lord say that. He was going to have to pray about it. I was furious, and withholding sex became a weapon. This led to more problems in our marriage. It went from me withholding to me feeling like I wasn't enough for him, but that was on me. I lit that flame.

A year later, I had gotten over the word that God had given me to move. My husband came home upset with one of the plant supervisors at his job. The supervisor was giving him a hard time and treating him unfairly. I didn't know at that time that God had also given him confirmation that we were to move, but he was indecisive about doing so. Things began to get harder for him at his job. One day, his supervisor said something to him that made him decide that day to put his notice in. His troubles caused him to obey, but again, by this time, I'm over it. I had no desire to move. I was a volunteer worker and manager at the ministry's grocery store. I was allowed to help in the process of getting it opened, stocked, and running. I went every day, faithfully, with no pay. I was happy and at peace. I did not want to move. My feelings were outweighing my faith.

We did eventually move that year, but it wasn't easy. When feelings override faith, it cancels out the power of the evidence not seen.

Whoredom is an emotional response. When you see visuals on TV, a whore or escort is created through a pimp who has convinced her or him that she or he is the most important person to the pimp. That they're valuable and precious. They are convinced that the pimp is the only one who is willing to give them anything they want. They are molded into becoming seductive, alluring, and attractive. Groomed into the business of attention. How to dress, how to walk, and even how to talk. Remember from chapter five, whoredom is defined not only as prostitution but also as faithless, unworthy, idolatrous practices or pursuits. Again, *faithless practices or pursuits*. Yes, we moved out of obedience, but we weren't of one accord. We both had a moment of faithlessness. My husband's faith wasn't active when I told him that God said to move. My faith wasn't active when he confirmed that God said to move. My stubbornness, pride, and feelings held me from becoming unified with the voice of God because I wanted what I wanted when I said it. Was it me or God? It was definitely God, but I was trying to stand in the place of God, making it all about me. Just like a pipe with a tiny crack, dripping. Drips of attention.

Before moving, my husband applied and interviewed for a full-time position at a local company in the area we were moving to and was hired. He was also working part-time at Sam's in our hometown and decided to put in a transfer to the local Walmart in the town we were moving to. He wanted to make sure we had enough funds to offset some of the moving costs when we arrived. We moved and got settled in fairly well. He went to the company where he had gotten hired at full-time, and the manager told him that he had decided to go with someone else for the job. We were shook! The part-time position at Walmart was paying only $6.75 an hour. We struggled for months. No one knew that we barely had food to eat. We ate a lot of syrup sandwiches and noodles. At this moment, all I can say is, "Thank you, Lord! You have been so good to us." We couldn't afford day care, so I got a job at a local gas station maybe three miles from our duplex. I worked at night because we had only one car. It was rough. This is Aimee's logic or opinion, but I felt our faith was being tried. Do we turn back, or do we stay and tough it out? There were a lot of up and down days. There is no doubt that during those years, we were only together because of our children. I can only speak for Aimee, and I know when I tapped out emotionally, it was pretty much over. For years, I begged for counseling to no avail. I hurt him badly, but he still stayed. I pushed him away, and he still stayed. I lied, and he knew it and still stayed.

He would tell me, "You will have to be the one that goes and files for divorce. I'm staying through the good and the bad." He loved me through my mess. He wasn't dwelling on my past or present. He was focused on my future. He invested in me. He wasn't looking to bear any risk of loss, because he knew his unconditional love would win. He was exemplifying the same type of love that Hosea had for Gomer. The same love God has for His children, Agape love.

CHAPTER 11
CHANGING FOCUS

Are you willing to love someone past their issues? I mean to the point that they can't deny that it's all love, not motives. To the point that the person can see you're not concerned about their past. You see only their future. I paid so much attention to what I didn't have that I lost focus on all I did have. All three of my stepfathers had good traits that we were able to grasp and build around. Our first stepdad had a close-knit family. People recognized them as one in the community. They each had their individual personalities. They were bold, hard workers that had a high regard for God and prosperity. We still recognize them as our family to this day. I know if I see any one of them, there will be plenty of laughter.

Our second stepfather was a kind and gentle soul. He didn't force his beliefs on us. He listened and genuinely cared about us. When he died, we were devastated. Our third stepfather came into our adult lives. He's our children's granddaddy. There's nothing he wouldn't do for our children. He taught my son how to fish, purchased his first fishing rod, laptop, and

cell phone, took him on ride-alongs, taught him how to operate a riding lawnmower, and so many other things. I had been
so blinded by my pain for so many years that I couldn't pull up
the good stuff.

As a child and through my teenage years, I felt like no one
could ever love me like my real dad. I longed for that daddy's
love. I remember being a guest speaker at a conference. I was
speaking about virtual reality versus reality. I made a comment that as female children, we tend to always want the attention of our daddy. You know, the daddy's girl. I went on to
say that I had a stepfather, but I felt like he couldn't love me
like my real father. That it wasn't possible for a stepfather to
love a daughter like that. One of the pastors came up to me
afterward and said, "That's a lie. I love all my children as my
own." I felt that. He doesn't even consider them "step" anything. They are his, and he is theirs. That was a lie the enemy
had placed in my head for years until I said, "Lord, will you be
my daddy?" My life begin to change. I still battled throughout
the years, hence this book, but I know beyond the shadow of
a doubt that I have a true and living Father who has grown
into everything in me. I wasted a lot of time focusing on the
naysayers, haters, foes, and opposition. I never took the time
to focus on the people that genuinely cared for me and pushed
me to be better. It was about three years ago when my mom
came to a women's conference in Tennessee. I was the night
speaker. I touched on the incident with my stepfather and how
she didn't leave him, but it didn't destroy our relationship. As

I was walking with her afterward, she looked at me and said, "Aimee, I want you to know that when all that happened with your stepfather, I couldn't leave right then because I didn't have anywhere for us to go. I had to save up some money. We were going to need shelter, furniture, and food. So I worked as hard as I could to make sure we had everything we needed." In chapter two, when I stated that we were moving and I didn't know why, this was why. She was building her funds to make the move. Nothing a child would understand, but as an adult, the picture became clearer. The enemy capitalized on the lie he was telling me that no one cared about me. That I was nothing. A nobody.

You do not have to submit to the lies of the enemy. You are more than your environment. You are stronger than you realize. With God on your side, you can be all he has created you to be. The enemy lied to Adam and Eve, disconnecting them from their place of worship. His trickery will have you going through life blind. Imagine yourself walking around with your eyes closed every day, everywhere. At home, you might do it with ease, but in unfamiliar places, you would more than likely begin to bump into a lot of things, causing some aches and pains along the way. Don't allow him to cause you to bruise yourself. Open your eyes and walk in the truth. The truth of God. When you hear "I can't" in your mind, tell yourself, "Yes, I can." All things, anything, can be done with Christ as your guide. Lean on Him. Trust in Him. Be willing to give your all to Him. You aren't defined by your past or present.

Think ahead. Think futuristically. Get in your Bible, and train your brain to unlearn some things. Approach the word of God openly, and let Him teach you. Psalms 119:18 (King James Version) states, "Open thou mine eyes, that I may behold wondrous things out of thy law." Psalms 119:1–18 (MSG) states, "You're blessed when you stay on course, walking steadily on the road revealed by God. You're blessed when you follow his directions, doing your best to find him."

That's right—you don't go off on your own; you walk straight along the road he set. You, God, prescribed the right way to live; now you expect us to live it. Oh, that my steps might be steady, keeping to the course you set; then I'd never have any regrets in comparing my life with your counsel. I thank you for speaking straight from your heart; I learn the pattern of your righteous ways. I'm going to do what you tell me to do; don't ever walk off and leave me. How can a young person live a clean life? By carefully reading the map of your Word. I'm single-minded in pursuit of you; don't let me miss the road signs you've posted. I've banked your promises in the vault of my heart so I won't sin myself bankrupt. Be blessed, God; train me in your ways of wise living. I'll transfer to my lips all the counsel that comes from your mouth; I n in gathering a pile of riches. I ponder every morsel of wisdom from you; I attentively watch how you've done it. I relish everything you've told me of life; I won't forget a word of it. Be generous with me, and I'll live a full life; not for a minute will I take my eyes off your road. Open my eyes so I can see what you show me of your miracle-wonders.

I opened my mouth and proclaimed to God that everything that He told me to say, I would say it. You have to get personal with God. Be open with him. He's that best friend you've been waiting for. It's a no-judgement zone with him. He forgives, corrects, and loves. Every time the enemy tries to hold something over your head or in your thoughts, remind him that he's a lie! Sometimes I think he forgets. Don't waste your days, months, and years dwelling on past mistakes you can't change. Move forward and do better. The ones that stay, stay. The ones that leave, leave. Focus solely on God. The ones that leave are the ones that he has removed, so move on. I've heard people say, "Don't burn bridges." Fact is, there may be a time when you're not the one starting the fire; it will be the ones walking away. Don't struggle to put it out. You will only get burned in the process. Keep moving forward.

CHAPTER 12
ACCOUNTABILITY

There comes a time in life when you have to take responsibility for all of your actions and thoughts. You cannot continue to place blame on everyone around you. Your actions were a choice. Yes, there may have been a cause for your choice, but the choice was still yours to make and do.

I made a choice to be angry, to hate, manipulate, cheat, lie, scheme, hurt, steal, and retaliate. I also made a choice to hold myself accountable for my actions. There's a quote about having to live with your choices. In my mind, "to live with" means to stay with, so nope, I refuse to stay there or live there. I'm moving on. We all have the right to move on to new days of grace. Ask God to forgive you, and use each day to work on forgiving yourself. Forgiveness of self becomes easier when you train yourself to extend that grace to other people who are dealing with their own individual issues. Lift up the downtrodden, the heavy hearts, the angry and misunderstood. Ask yourself what got them there and what you can do to give them hope that there is a way out of their current situation.

The way that God made a way for your escape, he'll do the same for others. "There hath no temptation taken you but such as is common to man: but God is faithful, who will not suffer you to be tempted above that ye are able; but will with the temptation also make a way to escape, that ye may be able to bear it" (1 Corinthians 10:13).

The Message Bible states it like this: "No test or temptation that comes your way is beyond the course of what others have had to face. All you need to remember is that God will never let you down; he'll never let you be pushed past your limit; he'll always be there to help you come through it."

Now, once you come through, don't go back to! It gets harder and harder every time you go back. Ask for and receive the gift of the Holy Spirit. He will guide you and comfort you. This is what worked for me. This is what I believe in. Find your belief. Dig deep, and come out of you! Come out of yourself. Stop being god to yourself. Separate your spirit from your inner man, your fleshly man, the part of you that craves darkness and evil. The whoredom part of you that weighs you down and pushes you backward.

I had to separate myself from me, people, places, and things. When I say "me," I mean things in me that were fleshly motivated. I couldn't talk how I used to talk. I couldn't listen to any and everything. This included certain preachers, entertainers, and music. I couldn't even look at certain TV shows. Those housewives' reality TV would have me all discombobulated. It's straight entertainment, but if you're not careful, it will become a part of you. You'll begin walking around with a chip on your shoulder and a big "I dare you" on your face and in your heart.

Accountability will make you hold yourself accountable for what you are allowing in your spirit. You and everyone connected to you will be able to tell what's in your spirit by what comes out of your mouth. For me, it was damage and death; damage to people and death within my spirit. The enemy will have you playing the blame game. Blaming everyone else for your downfalls. I would have the money I needed if Sally hadn't fired me from my job. I would've finished school if he hadn't gotten me pregnant. I would be further in my career if she weren't always holding me back. Blame, blame, blame turns to blah, blah, blah. Get up from blame! Dust yourself off and move forward. Your lack of financial increase, education, or anything that includes *you* can not be blamed on the opposition. You have the power within you to change your situation at any given moment. Hold yourself accountable. Rise up, and make the changes necessary to accomplish your dreams. Make your dreams your reality! You can do anything you put your mind to do. 1 John 4:4: "My dear children, you come from God and belong to God. You have already won a big victory over those false teachers, for the Spirit in you is far stronger than anything in the world" (*The Message* Bible). Rise up and show you're God-strong. Now unto him that is able to do exceedingly, abundantly above all that we ask or think, according to the power that worketh in us, go and be healed. Healed from your hurt and pain. Healed from doubt and confusion, loneliness and self-hate. Allow God to heal you as you walk. Walk close to him. Rest in him. He who knows all and sees all sees you! He created you, and he created you to win and prosper. Prosper as your soul prospers. How great of a Father we have that he looks down on us and calls us his children. There is nothing that we cannot have in Him. Allow him to use you for his glory. Your story. His glory! We will be complete and feel complete only through him. There's not a man or woman on this earth that will ever be able to complete you, but they can come along to enhance you as you enhance them, growing together in oneness with the Father and each other.

To my single people, know that the plan for your life is even greater. Never allow the enemy to lie and tell you that you are incomplete because you don't have a spouse or partner. God has created you for a specific work. Paul said that he wished we were all as he was. He was single. He had the freedom to work the kingdom as God had commissioned him to do. His only commitment was the kingdom of God. Make yourself available to and for the kingdom. Allow God to use you. Not man, but God. Go where he tells you to go. Build when he says to build, and keep moving. Enjoy the life of singleness. Singleness of oneness with the Father. Operate from the principles that he has set before you and laid out in His word for prosperity and good health. You are stronger than you realize. You are an overcomer. Love on people as He loves on you. Don't grow bitter and in want of what He hasn't finished creating for you. Don't rush the process. Let your patience increase. Work on you, and be ready if and when your person arrives!

In closing, allow yourself to be stripped of your issues. It will hurt. It may even leave a scar, but it will heal. I didn't have my biological father, but over the years, God placed strong spiritual fathers and men in my life who were encouraging and faithful in feeding God's people the words of the Lord. I'm grateful for my hardships and trials because they made me who I am today. I love me, and I love people. I haven't always been able to say that, but with a Father like the one I have, you can't help but do as he does. It's never too late to give yourself totally over to Him. He's here today. Allow him to have his way.

I pray that this book opens your eyes to the truth and fulfillment of God for your life. He knows the plans he has for you. Keep moving forward because His thoughts are good and not evil.

REVIEW

Grab a comfortable seat, get a cup or glass of your favorite drink, and get a snack; "He Married a Whore with Daddy Issues" is a don't-want-to-put-it-down book that will keep you on the edge of you seat waiting to see what could possibly happen to Aimee next! How will she handle it? Is anyone that cares in her corner? Which way will she turn now? All things are not as they seem.

This book is a good read for anyone but is especially excellent for the woman or man who is looking for and selling out to love in all the wrong places and ways.

Congratulations and God bless you, Aimee, on your first of many books.

—Pastor Lucille Hayes, Smith Temple Cumberland
Presbyterian Church of America, Mayfield, KY

ACKNOWLEDGEMENTS

None of this would be possible without God. I'm thankful and grateful. I want to thank my husband, Jeremy, for his patience and unconditional love toward me. To my children, Hannah and Joe'L, always remain humble and remember to be better than me. To my little big brother, Scott, for always being honest with me. To my sister, Ebbennie, for the perfect cover design. To my mentors, Mother Glenda Payne, Pastor Lucille Hayes, Elder Mary Parks, and Melody "HotChocolate" Collier, for your prayers, motivation, pushing, and whooping. To the teachers, planters, and waterers of my faith, the late Bishop James Mabry, Bishop C. L. Parks, and Dr. Jessie Webb, thank you for the unadulterated word of God.